A DUC

To Linda
with much affection
Hill.

DUOLOGUE SERIES 2

Canada Council
for the Arts

Conseil des Arts
du Canada

ONTARIO ARTS COUNCIL
CONSEIL DES ARTS DE L'ONTARIO

Guernica Editions Inc. acknowledges the support
of The Canada Council for the Arts.
Guernica Editions Inc. acknowledges the support
of the Ontario Arts Council.

WILLIAM ANSELMI

KOSTA GOULIAMOS

HAPPY SLAVES

A DUOLOGUE ON MULTICULTURAL DEFICIT

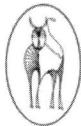

GUERNICA

TORONTO · BUFFALO · CHICAGO · LANCASTER (U.K.)

2005

Antonio D'Alfonso, editor
Guernica Editions Inc.
P.O. Box 117, Station P, Toronto (ON), Canada M5S 2S6
2250 Military Road, Tonawanda, N.Y. 14150-6000 U.S.A.

Distributors:
University of Toronto Press Distribution,
5201 Dufferin Street, Toronto, (ON), Canada M3H 5T8
Gazelle Book Services, White Cross Mills, High Town, Lancaster LA1 1XS U.K.
Independent Publishers Group,
814 N. Franklin Street, Chicago, Il. 60610 U.S.A.

First edition.
Printed in Canada.

Legal Deposit — Fourth Quarter
National Library of Canada
Library of Congress Catalog Card Number: 2005931733
Library and Archives Canada Cataloguing in Publication
Anselmi, William
Happy slaves : A duologue on multicultural deficit /
William Anselmi, Kosta Gouliamos. — 1st ed.
(Duologue series no. 2)
ISBN 1-55071-225-X
1. Elite (Social sciences) 2. Multiculturalism —Political aspects.
I. Gouliamos, Kosta II. Title. III. Series.
GN492.25.A54 2005 306.2
C2005-900829-6

ACKNOWLEDGEMENTS

As with any endeavour, *Happy Slaves: A Duologue on Multicultural Deficit* has been made possible, first and foremost, by those "fellow travellers" who have participated in this project, as well as Maria; Elena, Mitja and Daniil; Mikolai; they have, in different spaces, unfailingly supported us throughout, while our minds were wandering about, walking and talking.

Although Kosta and I assume all responsibility for everything that is said in this book, we owe more than just words to our friends. First of all, to Linda Donnelly for her dedication in transcribing what, at one point, must have seemed like alien sounds. We look upon her with grateful eyes for the hard work that cannot ever be fully compensated with these words. Thank you.

Of course, once our words went from tapes to paper, only one genial editor could have given them coherence. We humbly bow our heads to Karen Virag, whose craftmanship, patience and resilience have made this book better than Kosta and I would ever have imagined. Karen Virag is a rare editor indeed; if one word could cover this adventure it is to say, simply, how lucky we were.

We would also like to thank those close to us in Cyprus, Greece, Italy and Canada, who have given sustenance to our nomadic lives, while we played with words and ideas; they keep travelling with us, be they near or far.

HAPPY SLAVES

William Anselmi: Let's start by placing ourselves on a trajectory of ideas and exchanges and see where it takes us. When people meet, often the first question asked is: "Where are you from?"

Kosta Gouliamos: Well, since I know you and I'm familiar with your accent, I am not bothered by the question, because it's not being posed by a member of the so-called founding nations. If you were an Anglo-Saxon, I would be suspicious, because questions like that are always related to certain forms of racism and superiority complexes, which in turn lead to questions of power relations.

WA: Yes, the issue of power is ever present – that is, the person asking the question has already legitimized his or her own status with respect to the person to whom the question is posed. And the power imbalance is often covered up, or sweetened up, by the excuse that the person is just being curious or is showing interest in the other. I don't agree with that at all. I think such a question does not imply an interest in the other;

instead, it is meant to situate the other with respect to oneself in terms of power relations.

KG: I recently saw a magazine advertisement saying that "power is nothing without control." The advertisement showed the world-famous Brazilian soccer player Ronaldo advertising Pirelli tires. That commercial slogan – "Power is nothing without control" – applies perfectly to power relations in terms of ethnic backgrounds. The question "Where are you from?" clearly signifies a mechanism of control. When a person asks such a question, he or she clearly wants to control the relationship.

WA: So, in essence, there is never really a free exchange between people in so-called multicultural societies like Canada, precisely because there are all kinds of mechanisms at work that people might be naive or innocent enough to reproduce without any critical analysis. Perhaps without even realizing it, they set up relationships in which one is subjugated by the other. Nevertheless, I believe that there is no innocence in these types of questions because they establish a power imbalance and impede two people from entering freely into conversation.

KG: And this is precisely because of the political and social context of such a question, particularly in Canada, with its official system of multiculturalism, which in reality has become a system of culture based on folklore.

WA: Sometimes I am asked what happens if two people, recognizing each other's ethnic identity, ask each other that question – that is, "Where are you from?" – I would still contend that there is no innocence in it, because the power structures have been absorbed and repeated in the verbal exchange. In other words, there is always a hierarchy of power at work; so it doesn't matter if both these people recognize each other's ethnicity. I use the word "ethnic" in the sense that it is used in Canada, insofar as we distinguish it from the two so-called founding nations. It's always there, that power structure, the power relations; it's embedded in racism and revealed in racist discourse.

KG: And it is always reinforced by the state apparatus and, in particular, by various government departments that perpetuate the bicultural system even though there is an established multiculturalism policy. As an example, let's look at the Canada Council. Sometimes, in order to prove that Canada is an open society, the Canada Council gives grants to writers or, in another way of putting it, they "allow" some writers to enter the bicultural power structure. This reveals a control mechanism at work, and I think we should concentrate on it because we have to understand the role of the writer as an intellectual within this particular frame.

WA: But before we go on, let's go back in time. These cultural control mechanisms appeared on the Canadian scene with the Trudeau government and were, in a way, an attempt to recuperate and redefine the reality of Canada. Prior to the Second World War, Canada was made up of defined and specific ethnic groups already producing their own cultural material – newspapers, books, plays and so on – in their own language. By the time the Second World War began, these practices stopped, or at least became dormant. Then, by the 1960s, governments everywhere were being threatened by changing social mores. The highly visible multi-ethnic component of Canada started to seem threatening to the status quo and had to be neutralized. When identity comes from below, that is, when it is expressed at the level of ordinary people, it acquires its own democratic status. The Canadian government, beginning with Trudeau right through to Mulroney, recuperated and neutralized the dimension of ethnic reality by passing the Multiculturalism Act,[1] which meant that from that time forward, ethnicity and identity were going to be regulated and imposed from above. Thus, the specific guidelines and structures . . .

KG: . . . Which are power structures . . .

WA: . . . For the representations of these ethnic groups are laid down by the state. In other words, identity does not come from below anymore, from the actual ethnic groups – it's imposed from above. And now we're back to the idea of mechanisms of control, which are so insidious, because they are about denouncing, neutralizing, forgetting, and erasing the idea of a part of Canadian history. The result is that ensuing generations and intellectuals have bought into the idea of multiculturalism imposed by the state. And this is the essential paradigm by which we are to govern ourselves. I say "govern" in an ironic sense, of course.

KG: As we talked about in our book *Elusive Margins*, we can observe the continuation of the neutralization politics of Trudeau right through to the commercialization of multiculturalism during the Mulroney era. What we end up with is a typical integration of the political and financial or commercial apparatus.

WA: Under the name of multiculturalism.

KG: Exactly. But let me go back to the point that I made previously. I think that, within this historical frame that you referred to, we have to reconsider the role of an ethnic writer as an intellectual in Canadian or North American society. I strongly believe that writers often become mere bureaucrats of art. And this is exactly what a power system wants: artists must become passive and must learn to speak in the language of power.

WA: In other words, they repeat internalized power structures *ad nauseum*.

KG: Precisely. It's a process of neutralization that requires us to reconsider the role of intellectuals, not just in North America, but globally.

WA: Let's return to the idea of how so-called ethnic writers are recruited and neutralized. You mentioned the agency of the state and of state institutions, like the Multicultural Department,[2] the Canada Council, the various R and D departments and so on. One way that these organizations recruit and neutralize ethnic identities is through granting specific recognition in the form of awards, like the Governor General's Award. Nino Ricci's novel *Lives of the Saints*, which won the Governor General's Award in 1991, is a double-edged sword. First, it does precisely what you described – it gives back a passive identity to its ethnic protagonists – and, second, it reinforces the stereotype by which that ethnic group is considered by the dominant culture. Now the two dominant discourses that constitute official biculturalism – the Anglophone and Francophone – are actually minorities, as any map of the ethnic composition of Canada will show you.[3] But neither of these two ethnocultural groups considers itself ethnic.

KG: That's because they are part of . . .

WA: . . . The dominant discourse. Yes. They are the ones who carry on certain traditions, maintain a certain status. In *Elusive Margins*, we tried to redefine terms and look beyond a bicultural state to a multicultural federation.

KG: I like the word "transcultural."

WA: Yes. Transcultural federation. But the notion of authenticity becomes a problem. Certain writers who are identified as ethnic are authentic or have the means of authentic expression and are tied to the identity-formation processes of their own ethnocultural background. But they are neutralized and the questions arise, why and how do authentic expressions get neutralized and voided of their content? Let's start with the Canadian literary canon. Margaret Atwood, in her 1972 book *Survival*, talks about a number of writers, but specifically states that she avoids ethnic writers because they are not permanent to Canada.[4] Now that is an interesting political position; if you separate her words from the context, it's clear what mechanisms of control are at work. Even in the reprint of this anthology in the mid-1990s, she still refused to recognize the presence of ethnic writers. So here we go again with a canon that insists that it has the right to define what being Canadian means. This insistence is obviously a means of control that once again marginalizes, or expels, any other form of production. That is, any production that does not fit into the mainframe of the representation of Canadian identity.

KG: But the question remains, what is the role of the intellectual in our time, in our society? I would say that Margaret Atwood is a very good example of control management. She reinforces what we know about power relations and the way the Canadian state works in terms of culture. Are Canadian identity, Canadian culture defined solely as Anglo-Saxon Protestant or French-Canadian Catholic? If we consider the passivity of state-imposed multiculturalism, the folkloric approach to multiculturalism, and all the practices that reinforce passive identity, we are left with a void of critical discourse. This void gives space to racism or to a strong support for the status quo, which is often reinforced by academia or writers. Take as an example Robertson Davies' comments of six or seven years ago about how great the monarchy is.[5] What I am getting at is that we have to acknowledge the existence of exclusionary politics, and Mr. Davies and Ms. Atwood represent exclusionary politics. They are part of the state cultural apparatus, and I must add that it is quite dangerous, particularly in the new millennium, to have discourses with racist . . .

WA: . . . Discourses based on race?

KG: Yes. In fact, these kinds of discourse reveal the true level of intellectual discourse in the bicultural Canadian context. And, despite its pretense to the contrary, I would suggest that Canadian society is not an open society, but a very closed society. If you follow the dictates of official biculturalism and the canon, but you are not part of the governing power structure, then you can be sure that your identity will be consumed, nullified.

WA: With a little help from the mainstream media. Let's consider what has been published recently, especially in the *National Post*. One columnist, Diane Francis, suggested to the ever-ready-to-consume public that ethnicity has become a burden on the Canadian identity, a burden that used to be tolerated, but that now needs to be eliminated. Francis has frequently suggested acts of exclusion based on race, which she boils down to a "problem of management." For her, the solution to immigration is simple: racism has to be internalized within the ethnic group. It's like a process of self-cannibalism, of consumption of oneself. With her repeated attacks against "otherness," against ethnicity, and her description of immigrants as "sleazes coming from muck" – I'm quoting from one of their articles – she encourages ethnic groups to neutralize themselves by a process self-hatred. We have come to the point that it is no longer necessary to eliminate difference with edicts from above because you can eliminate them from . . .

KG: . . . Within.

WA: Exactly. This is what I would call "cultural genocide," but by state-controlled mechanisms of oppression and exclusion. Diane Francis is one of many people writing for the then Conrad Black owned chain of newspapers who show this practice at work.[6]

KG: Your point about cultural genocide is right. For me, it's a continuation of the other genocide that took place centuries ago, when the Anglos and the French came to this country and systematically killed the native population. Is it possible to differentiate this cultural genocide, the extermination of the "different," from the political or the ethnic genocide that took place centuries ago?

WA: What we must not forget, though, is the way the Canadian state has conveniently used ethnicity for the construction of a certain type of society. And now that society seems to have been more or less achieved, it is necessary to eliminate the ethnic. I'm not talking about assimilation as ethnic groups move towards the centre. I'm talking about the total elimination of those groups as undesirables, as the different. What is necessary is their elimination, their removal from Canadian history, from Canadian reality, from Canadian representation. What is allowed to remain is not content, but a *pro forma* state of superficial consumption. For example, we have products like Mediterranean sauce. There is no more Italy or Spain or Cyprus or Greece, but something generic – Mediterranean – which carries a hint of exoticism, while at the same time removes the particularity of ethnic reality.

KG: I would like to go back to the point you made regarding the power that the bicultural Canadian identity exercises with respect to ethnic background. For me, it's quite important to see the relationship between the Canadian state and the established writers in Canada. We have to find out what their role is, what their connection or interconnection is and how Canada reinforces such writers as Atwood or Robertson Davies or Michael Ondaatje, who comes, of course, from an ethnic background, although he entered the official bicultural landscape.

WA: The culturalscape.

KG: Yes. What are the connections? What kind of grants do these people get from the state? What is their connection to dominant mass media apparatuses? To publishing houses?

WA: And to the distribution of this material?

KG: To the distribution of power. We have to see

their connection to the distribution of power when it comes to agencies of power.

WA: Okay. Let's try to answer these questions by referring to a specific work: *Selling Illusions* by Neil Bissoondath. Here we have a cultural agent – let's call him that – with a non-Anglo, non-French ethnic background, who internalizes the neutralizing aspect of multiculturalism (and achieves instant notoriety and success) with a book that is full of problematic, unsubstantiated statements and an untenable ideological position. In this book, Bissoondath suggests that multiculturalism is an illusion, and a destructive illusion at that, because, for one thing, there is no possibility of grounding the experience into something solid. Obviously, we have to point out that (a) the book is a direct cultural attack against immigration itself, or migration, or what we like to call "nomadism," which is really the history of humanity; (b) it is a deconstructing from within of the multicultural discourse by showing how representatives of multiculturalism are co-opted; they then denounce multiculturalism as a failure; and (c) it reinforces the idea of biculturalism as the sole agent of representation. And this ties in with what I was saying before, that, again, it is calling for the disappearance of the different in Canada. Cultural genocide.

KG: Let's see how the process of cultural genocide

takes place in Canada. First of all, Ms. Atwood or Mr. Davies cannot exercise cultural genocide alone. They have to have a mechanism that supports their discourse, and this mechanism works within the parameters of cultural hegemony. Cultural hegemony is not just an abstract concept; it is concrete. Let's see what's going on in Canada when it comes to the reinforcement of bicultural discourses. There are opinion leaders in mass media and government departments – bureaucrats, in other words – and there are cultural think tanks, particularly within the universities – English departments, French departments, even social and political science departments – that reinforce the *status quo*, thus reducing the possibility of critical discourse and the airing of other viewpoints. Therefore, the space is left wide open for racism and for certain neo-fascist practices, which both of us have experienced in our university careers.

WA: That makes me think about what happened at Carleton University during the academic year 1997-98, with the closing of the School of Languages, Literatures, and Comparative Literary Studies. The university administration, through the Dean of Arts and Social Sciences, and with the go-ahead by the president of the university, Mr. Richard Van Loon, characterized the School as "problematic" and advocated for its abolition. But how did the School begin in the first place?

Well, it was actually part of a strategy for the new millennium that supported the existence and teaching of various languages – Italian, German, Spanish, Russian – as well as comparative literature and classics.

KG: Greek?

WA: Greek was part of classics. However, by the end of the summer of 1998, we were more or less told that we shouldn't exist. I saw this as a demonstration of revenge and hostility within a broader political context: Ontario and its neo-conservative government. At first, the explanation for the closing of the school was that they didn't know how we fit in, how we belonged. Then, they started using an economic discourse, claiming that the School was actually losing money to the tune of $500,000. We ourselves discovered that there was a financial mistake made by the administration – we were actually $88,000 in the black. This did not alter the course of the process at all. In fact, the University administration came back a week later and admitted that the original figure was wrong; we were only $250,000 in the red. Ironically, an interview with Carleton's president that appeared in the November issue of the *Charlatan*, the student newspaper, identified the so-called economic problems as minor. Finally, in the first week of December 1997, the School was closed down.

I should also mention how the media behaved. In an editorial in the *Ottawa Citizen*, which is part of the Conrad Black chain, the programs and the people who taught them were characterized, and this is verbatim, as "poorly trained people teaching mediocre programs." So there was already the suggestion that the languages of the School of Languages were not only unnecessary, but "unprofessional." What's more, during a meeting with colleagues from other departments and faculties, we were identified as the "gangrene" of Carleton University.

This is the background behind the closing of the School. From my point of view, there was no necessity for the School to close, and I see the closure as an attempt to eliminate the different languages and cultures and literatures that are represented within the so-called multicultural state of Canada. Carleton should actually be really proud for being part of the avant-garde, the first to establish the structure for the elimination of languages and, therefore, for the complete reinstatement of the monolithic bicultural state.

KG: I can see the whole university practice as a concrete example of cultural genocide. Something similar happened, as you know very well, a few years ago, in 1994-95 at the University of Ottawa, when the Department of Communication didn't want to establish a critical studies approach. And the students established a critical movement in response. They asked for more critical studies to the point that the university bureaucrats felt threatened and the group ended up dissolving. So, things repeat themselves. Cultural genocide and the absence of critical studies and critical discourse reinforce the notion of cultural hegemony at all levels of social, political and cultural life. The question is, where are the voices of resistance in such environments? How can they be heard? How can they be recognized, not in terms of the cult of celebrity, but rather . . .

WA: . . . In the exercise of critical faculties?

KG: And if we don't have a politics of resistance to the exercise of cultural genocide that happens in Canada, then the question is, Are we moving into an absolute authoritarian cultural state that only pretends that it is polyphonic and democratic and open?

WA: I would say that we live in a totalitarian state, but the totalitarian state mechanism has differentiated itself from the crude, abrasive totalitarian regimes. It has refined itself into a mechanism that gives you, to quote Mr. Bissoondath, "the necessary illusions," the belief that, à la Leibnitz, this is the best of all possible worlds.[7] Take, for example, the formulations that surround "selling" to the public the notion that global capitalism is good for the poor. An article appeared in *The Economist* in 2002 that quotes, wrongly, the Catalan economist Xavier Sala-i-Martin. *The Economist* article states that, in the twenty years, the percentage of people living at $2 per day has gone from 44 percent to 8 percent, whereas, according to Sala-i-Martin, the percentage is not 8 but 18. So, on the surface, global capitalism, as expressed in *The Economist,* would appear to be a positive thing. Yet some questions remain.

I read an article in *Il Manifesto* that shows how numbers, which you think would be neutral, can be deceptive. Take a group of 100 persons, each with an average income of, say $5,000 per year. If one of those persons becomes a millionaire, the average income goes up dramatically (to $14,950). In reality, 99 persons still make only $5,000 per year. That is the beauty of how numbers can be manipulated. Few have shown how global capitalism is actually stimulating an increase in criminal profits through drugs and off-shore investments. Jean de Maillard, a French magistrate, presents an irrefutable reading of this in his *Le marché fait sa loi.* Yet we are content with the uncritical acceptance that this is the best possible world, and many are proud that Canada gets recognized by the U.N. as the best possible country in the world in terms of good life.

KG: I'm curious. Who or what mechanism establishes the criteria for deciding what is a good life?

WA: The rankings are based on strict capitalist criteria and preclude any aspects of the quality of life that do not fit that capitalist model. In the end, it does not describe real life, or the lifeworld . . .

KG: . . . But it does describe the deathworld. And if we consider passivity a manifestation of the good life, then . . .

WA: . . . Then we agree that Canada should be number one in the world.

KG: Yes.

WA: Getting back to the notion of totalitarianism, I call Canada totalitarian because, first of all, the mechanism of identity affirmations has been so altered that society becomes passive or self-consumptive or self-cannibalistic. There is a film by Jim Jarmusch called *Dead Man*, featuring scenes of ethnic cannibalism that illustrate this practice at work.[8] In Canada, what looks like freedom of expression and representation is really a coded mechanism of alienation, because all the different apparatuses are orchestrated, perhaps in a monolithic way, such that identity is subdued by its own consumption. In other words, identity is altered from something authentic into something that is readily consumable and readily sellable. In terms of the structures of the lifeworld, everything around seems to reinforce one and the same pattern; that is, the media, the cultural industry, entertainment industry, and so on, all replicate and represent one and the same discourse – artificial consumption of artificial desires. And the actual political mechanism of representation cannot but represent what is already given. So there is no possibility of critical discourse – the encoded mechanism only allows what has already been formed to be represented. We live in a vacuous state whose social and economic reality is full of mirrors. That's why I contend that Canadian totalitarianism is refined; it gives the appearance of democracy, but in reality represents one model, one pseudo-reality. The advertising industry is a good example of an industry that understands this very well. I find slogans like "Freedom Fifty-Five" [a retirement investment scheme] or the 6/49 lottery pitch – "Imagine the Freedom" – perverted, because they alter the meaning of words. In these two examples, "freedom" is connected solely to financial status. It's the same semantic game that appears in George Orwell's *Nineteen Eighty-Four*, where war is peace; peace is war. This is what I mean by refined totalitarianism.

KG: I disagree with you when it comes to the definition of the Canadian state as totalitarian. I believe that Canada has all the symptoms of a liberal oligarchic state in the sense that Castoriadis uses it.[9] It's not totalitarian because, first of all, by definition, there are two founding nations that never became an integrated state. They are still fighting with each other. Therefore we still don't have a monolithic model.

WA: But when you say they're fighting each other, you know very well that this pseudo-polarized position is only operational insofar as it completely erases ethnic representations from the media discourse. What has happened in Canada in the last thirty years is this continuous representation of two realities – the French and the English – that end up legitimizing each other and continuously excluding others.

KG: It includes all the exclusionary politics that we have talked about in both of our books. No question about it. Although we have to say that the state, the model state, works in a relative state of autonomy. I think it's very hard to say that Canada is a totalitarian state. I think it's a democratic oligarchy, which I define as a state in which relatively autonomous groups, agencies in other words, work together to exclude others or erase histories, such as ethnic histories, but at the same time, in order to prove that they are democratic, they allow some ethnic discourses to enter their space and become part of their own reality. In this day and age, truly totalitarian regimes are difficult to maintain unless they are completely independent and don't care about anyone else. The Canadian state gives the impression and to some extent exercises a politics of interest, but this interest is commercial or financial, as you noted before. It's something that becomes sellable.

WA: So we have to find the origins of this model of oppression, which you contend is not totalitarian but does oppress.

KG: It is a model of oppression certainly, but this model of oppression is not similar to, say, fascist Germany, or some other totalitarian state, like the former Soviet Union with its gulags, or the Taliban in Afghanistan. We're really not talking about those kinds of things. Instead, we're talking about more refined kinds of oppression that are more insidious, but we don't want to understand that we are slaves.

WA: We're happy slaves.

KG: We are happy slaves, for sure. Anyway, whether Canada is a totalitarian or a democratic oligarchy state, the question is, what is the role of intellectuals? I would like to go back to the two questions that I raised earlier to understand the *modus operandi* of a state multicultural system. Now, for me, intellectuals have shown a poverty of commitment on many levels. First, where is the voice of resistance? And how can this voice of resistance be recognized? Even if we talk about critical discourse, we must include praxes. We cannot stay in the realm of abstract expression. We have to go somewhere; we have to put theory into practice. We have to make things move.

WA: But intellectuals depend on the sources or tools available to them in order to discern truth. And sometimes the tools are limited. If we go back, in what I call this process of refinement of oppression, we start the 1990s with the statement by Francis Fukuyama about "the end of History."[10] Fukuyama represents a neo-conservative, right-wing points of view that argued for the elimination of terms such as "oppression," "emancipation," "Hegelian dialectics," and that contended that the so-called liberal democracies, à la the United States, had won their final triumph. Other systems, other ways of thinking and viewing the world didn't matter anymore. So if your contention that there is a poverty of commitment among intellectuals is true, perhaps we can put it down to a system that sees everything as absolutes and that discourages critical thought and reflection. It is almost impossible to describe a world that has lost certain words or certain categories and tools of analysis, and where the historic twentieth century opposition between the left and the right has been vanquished by one model of right-centre control. Let's take Italy as an example. In the 1990s, a government of the so-called Ulivo coalition [the Olive Coalition][11] was elected. It was made up principally of members of the old Italian Communist party. You might think that it would be progressive but in reality it was the opposite and enacted right-wing practices and policies. I see the poverty you are talking about as a global poverty of analysis, critical ability, and representation. I think that intellectuals are responsible for the world and that they partake of the world using the tools made available to them. And this illustrates what Marcuse used to call the unidimensional reality.[12] We do believe that we live in a unidimensional world, a world of constantly changing, constantly consumable images, and even if there are pockets of resistance here and there (I'm only thinking of the Western world), they aid the mechanism of entering into the live world discourse. You could ask, What about the World Wide Web? And I would answer that the Web offers the possibility of altering discourses, but in reality it tends to be limited to promoting consumerism. Furthermore, not everybody has access to it. In this world that we consume, intellectuals have also lost, for better or worse, the power they carried in the eighteenth and nineteenth centuries. In fact, the intellectual today is really a strange figure without any real authority. His or her means of analysis have been depleted by the capitalistic system, and the role has been overshadowed by Hollywood and the cult of celebrity, which grant certain public figures the right to represent and speak for others. I guess there are examples of intellectuals who have something interesting to say that applies to the lifeworld – Noam Chomsky, for example – but overall most of them seem like puppets.

KG: I don't think that intellectuals are strange figures. Let's look at two concepts of intellectuals; one, the concept of the *organic intellectual,* developed by Gramsci[13] and the other, the *questioning intellectual,* developed by Montaigne.[14] I would like to add another category. I contend that in literary, academic and political realms there are intellectuals who have been transformed into instruments or agents who rationalize oppression. They become entrepreneurs, actors of pop culture but, really, the only thing they achieve is temporary fame.

WA: Andy Warhol's famous fifteen minutes of fame, right?

KG: Precisely. And to add to Gramsci and Montaigne, I would like to introduce the concept of *programmed intellectuals.*[15] Sometimes the state has to establish agencies, like think tanks, to serve the interest of dominant discourses. The result is programmed intellectuals who reflect the strategic objectives of the dominant discourse and are programmed to perform specific roles and to support the interests of dominant powers. The Fraser Institute is an example of one of these right-wing think tanks.[16]

WA: You define intellectuals as passive agents. But are they so passive that they can't see how they're being used as instruments of domination, or do they actively collaborate in this?

KG: It works in both ways. It's not just a passive exercise or an active exercise. And, really, it doesn't make any difference, because both cases lead to the state of instrumental rationality. They've been transformed into such a state, and that's why they have become entrepreneurs, motivated by their own personal interests.

WA: Yes, but could they have done otherwise? We live in a world in which everything is turned into a commodity, ideas included. And the *modus operandi* of this commodification is the erasure of differences, the bringing together of everything under a hegemonic umbrella, so even the intellectuals have been trapped; they have nothing to sell but their ideas. However, the market is looking only for certain types of ideas. Not everything can be sold.

KG: If we consider the intellectual as something strictly theoretical that deals with writing and papers and books and ideas, then, yes, we can observe the process of commodification at work. However, intellectuality requires one more thing: it requires the transformation from theory into praxis, into an active praxis. If we don't have that, then writers and intellectuals become mere bureaucrats. We go back to . . .

WA: . . . An administered knowledge.

KG: Yes.

WA: A limited kind of knowledge. Bounded knowledge.

KG: Bounded knowledge. Intellectuals certainly are part of the bounded knowledge; they are even producers and distributors of this knowledge. What is missing in these times is an active praxis on the part of intellectuals. In other words, intellectuals do not participate in the social and political process. Now, consider two particular wars of the last two years: the Gulf War and the war in the former Yugoslavia, in Kosovo. What was the reaction of the intellectuals? What was their involvement in these two major events? A war that was fought not for the protection of human rights, but for the protection of the oil industry or some other capital interest. Intellectuals were completely absent on the academic and political fronts. And I am talking both about the intellectuals of the establishment and the ethnic critics as well. In other words, we heard only . . .

WA: . . . Silence.

KG: Silence.

WA: A post-something silence. Or a post-something censorship.

KG: In *Voltaire's Bastards*, John Ralston Saul describes very well how the Canadian establishment exercises its own power. I would like to understand what caused this paralysis. And furthermore, I would like to understand how and what environments produce and reproduce the mechanism of silence.

WA: I can give you a specific example. Intellectuals have failed to recognize and to intervene in the U.N. actions in Kosovo because, in Canada, the situation was never considered a war; it was an intervention in favour of human rights, following the American dictum. This shows a complete misunderstanding of multiculturalism, because multiculturalism in Canada exists on a surface level; it doesn't evoke the idea of connection with other ethnic groups throughout the world, which is what true multiculturalism is all about. So the failure of multiculturalism to speak out in the absence of public debate and to show that the U.N. actions in Kosovo were acts against multiculturalism, under the guise of the protection of human rights, reveals the failure of critical ability and analysis within a self-declared multicultural context. In other words, state-imposed multicul-turalism is consumed at the surface level, and it's reconducted back into folklore, dancing and . . .

KG: . . . Food

WA: Right. The Gulf war reveals a deeper problem: during the 1940s, several ethnic groups were interned by the Canadian government, prominent among them Italians, Germans, and Ukrainians. And it wasn't just people from these countries but people of those ethnic origins who were actually Canadian citizens that were interned. The state literally declared some of its own citizens as ene-mies. The story of Japanese internment is fairly well known, but the internment of other ethnic groups is not.

Now how is this connected to the Gulf War? Because during the Gulf War, people of Arabic origin, or who looked like Arabs, were being harassed by the RCMP in an eerie re-enactment of the same process that took place during the 1940s. Because these racist acts were never chal-lenged, the process remained alive and well and can be repeated at any given time, just as at any given time any given citizen can be designated as the enemy within. In other words, you can be "de-statusised." Now this brings up a question of praxis, which brings me back to Ms. Diane Fran-cis, who stated in an article in the *Post* that political refugees constitute a category of criminals who should be eliminated from Canada and that Canadian citizenship should be revoked from criminals.[17] But I will pose what may seem an absurd question – *reductio ad absurdum* – how far back do we go? Because if we are to remove citizenship from criminals, then many Canadians wouldn't be here today. Many among the first wave of immigration from England and France were criminals, prostitutes and so on, all banished to the colonies. Many of us should lose our citizenship according to Miss Francis. I'm making an absurd joke, but I think it strikes at the core of what is entailed within this process of deciding who belongs.

KG: Definitely there are manifestations and fixations here that apply even to the recent war in Kosovo and that mirror to a great extent the kind of experience the Serbs now face. What struck me is that when the U.S.A. moved against, let's say, Serbia, they found, as with Saddam Hussein in Iraq, someone to demonize: Slobodan Milosevic. And in so doing, they personalize history. And they excuse their actions by saying that they want to protect human rights, even though they are pretty selective about whose rights are worthy of being protected. They seem to pretty much ignore human rights abuses in Cyprus . . .

WA: . . . Or East Timor.

KG: It is very important to scrutinize the actions of the G-8, which in some ways is replacing the United Nations – a dangerous thing.[18] However, even the United Nations Security Council eliminates or erases histories in a highly selective way. They try to impose pseudo-constitutional solutions in both Cyprus and East Timor just to show the rest of the world that they care, but the solutions they are suggesting or imposing have no meaning, because they are contrary to human rights and to the desire of the people themselves.

WA: This calculated fomenting of international conflicts is really just part of the world order envisioned and invoked by George Bush, which involves creating or exacerbating conflict abroad for the interests of capital to resolve violent situations somewhere in the world – it therefore acts as both a masking and a "demasking" process – and to maintain control within his own society. Leaders like Bush realize that people's opinions are easily directed and manipulated toward specific areas, such as potential conflict. Therefore, other problems in society are minimized by distracting the public. This is another obvious mechanism of control.

KG: Or control management exercised in various areas of socio-political and cultural life. The question that we have to answer is, How do intellectuals react to this kind of post-colonial practice? I strongly believe that if we start in Canada, we will see that it is impossible for a state that exercises post-colonial practices within its own territory not to exercise the same kind of policy outside its own territory.

WA: In fact, this type of failure points to the fact that post-colonial discourse is another invention, a rhetorical invention, by which we seem to have moved further ahead in terms of being critical about our history, but which, in turn, becomes another discourse of control, because it gives power to those who already have it.

KG: Or it perpetuates that power.

WA: Yes. In a way, it's a process that contains both its alpha and omega, its beginning and end. And it creates its own super-dialectical discourse, but it's always contained. It is manufactured, pervasive, and it eliminates true critical discourse. It seems to contain both extremes within itself, but it's always managed from above.

KG: That's why whatever we describe relates to the concept that I mentioned before: programmed intellectuals. I assert again that the agencies of power in literary, academic, political, financial, commercial or cultural realms operate to perpetuate control management. And in doing so, it is quite impossible for them to go against forced colonial practices. Of course, we can observe different degrees of reaction, but this comes from a bourgeois humanitarian appreciation. It reminds me of the type of movement that was developed at the beginning of this century in Italy: *verismo*.[19] You know that the bourgeoisie at the turn of the century in Italy had a certain degree of humanitarian appreciation . . .

WA: What one might call a socialistic understanding.

KG: Yes. It gave the impression that there was a need to . . .

WA: . . . Better the conditions of the exploited.

KG: And I believe that to a great extent the same thing happened here. It's like a photocopy of history.

WA: Yes, a history that continues to duplicate itself, and therefore it's not history anymore, but a continuum. A vicious circular continuum.

KG: This is a kind of a Viconian concept of *corsi e ricorsi storici*.[20]

WA: Now to give a concrete illustration, let's look at Canada's intervention in Kosovo. We saw the rise in this country of two factions: the pro-war faction, which was the Canadian government, and the anti-war faction, which was vocalized largely by one person, Senator Doug Roche, whose motto was "stop the bombing now," a sincere, but uncritical, reaction to the war. It's one thing to simply declare that the bombing should stop; what we really need to do is analyze the situation. Within the system, there were the pro and con sides, both of which are contained within the same process. The result of this conflation is that the possibility of society making its own critical analysis and judgement is voided; any possibility of a true, authentic intervention into a state's actions is nullified because the answers were already supplied. The polarized opinions left no room or possibility for critical analysis. The sickness gives life to its own antibodies, which it contains and manages.

KG: That's why we are talking about the relative autonomy of the state. The maintenance of a dominant discourse works according to its ability to void opposing discourses. Why did the cultural apparatuses, including ethnic communities, become so silent?[21] What will be the result of this silence in the near future? What kind of paradigm or model will the new generations have to resist oppression?

WA: It teaches the new generations to be passive and dormant and to allow the state to manage itself. It reminds me of the Italian notion of *contentino*, a little bit of a reward so as to attain the status quo without changing its parameters or recognizing the process. With respect to the Italian-Canadian context, why have these problems not been addressed by certain Italian-Canadian critics and intellectuals? Perhaps because acting within a particular ethnic space is comfortable and familiar, even though it serves to ghettoize identity. And ghetto identities can never open up to other ghetto identities and, therefore, on the surface, they seem to be self-protecting mechanisms that continue to produce various cultural products, like books, magazines and so on. But the ghettoization means that differences are self-contained and self-administered through the oppressive effect of state-imposed multiculturalism. Ethnicity becomes a consumer item or an entertainment at the level of literary and cultural praxis.

KG: Similar things can be observed in other ethnic communities, including the Anglo and the French-Canadian. I think, though, that we have to go above and beyond such a practice. We have to recognize that there is an accelerated ethnic ghettoization process in place, not just in Canada but all over the world. This process is imposed by the G-8 and in particular by Anglo-American interests that try to impose the state multicultural paradigm in other areas of the world. It is almost as though, since they cannot export exotic foods, they export conflict and division. If we look at history as an ongoing, as opposed to a linear, process, we can see that it is a practice of divide, consume and conquer. The British empire, from Malaysia, India, Cyprus, Ireland, to Canada, to name a few, is an excellent example of this. Such a practice went over quite well during the war in Kosovo, where they tried to establish an enhanced post-colonial practice that resulted in a hybrid compartmentalized state. And the ultimate ghetto state that they wanted to establish there is based on division and conflict. We must acknowledge that the Western world exports a fabricated multiculturalism to other countries even as they export, let's say, sex, violence, racism, oppression, and military equipment.

WA: And obedience and subservience.

KG: Precisely.

WA: What we want to do is unravel the Gordian knot of the purported difference between the American melting pot model and the Canadian mosaic. Why? Because in the end they achieve the same thing. In a melting pot, the individual is immediately voided of historicity and roots in order to belong to a hegemonic, non-historical representation. The mosaic model, the Canadian model, voids the idea of heritage, roots and belonging to a difference because identity is imposed from above and becomes reduced to food and folk dance. Therefore, both models operate by eliminating historicity and roots. Certainly, as immigrant families have children and their children have children, there is a self-willed renunciation of belonging to a difference and a concomitant assimilation into the dominant paradigm, which, given the reality of Canada, is usually an Anglophone reality.

KG: Which at the same time creates a high degree of acculturation.

WA: Yes. We've already talked about Neil Bissoondath's vision of multiculturalism, and I think it stands once again as an example.

KG: However, the accelerated ghetto process that is fabricated by Anglo-American interests provides one more thing. It provides not just technologies of oppression but technologies of death. For example, the people in Kosovo were on the wrong end of 235 kilos of depleted uranium. During the Gulf war, again, the Anglo-Americans dropped close to 290 pounds of the same product.[22] And the really amazing thing is that the whole time, the world was watching everything happen on TV. We are witnesses of a tele-war.

WA: Also "spectacularization," which voids the meaning for the consuming public because the war becomes a show, a mere spectacle, and nothing else. Then, of course, there is the perversion of language: the Americans and British dropping bombs on the ancient city of Baghdad and killing women and children became Operation Desert Storm, making the whole thing sound like a fun and exciting video game. The war in Kosovo was an "intervention," an innocuous sounding word that masked the really terrible things that were happening there. Then, after the war, the U.N. imposed an embargo on Iraq that brutalized the country.[23]

KG: As we enter the new millennium and talk about human rights and civilization, we see a big contradiction within the neo-liberal states. On one hand, the Anglo-American states would like to talk about human rights and democracy; on the other, they exercise norms and practices of oppression.

WA: But let's not forget that this contradiction is resolved by the spectacle.

KG: The spectacle, yes. That reminds me of something. A writer, I believe it was Mary Melfi, in her "O Canada" poems, once said that civilization can be reduced to a menu. This is very fitting when we think of the multicultural identity in Canada. But getting back to the notion of how control is exercised, the Anglo-American state – not just the U.S.A. – establishes a system of a control to stifle all voices of reaction. The fact that people – like Norman Mailer, who claimed in a newspaper interview that he was against the American intervention in Kosovo – were protesting meant absolutely nothing. Why? Because it's a matter of superficial protest. No action results from it. What has Mailer done to stop Clinton? What has Atwood done to stop Chrétien? Sometimes it seems to me that Canada is a state with a voice, but without language. If Canada does not cut the umbilical cord with London or Washington or even Paris, and renounce the monarchy and Commonwealth, it becomes a meaningless entity. We have European union, we have NAFTA, I still don't understand . . .

WA: We have the Commonwealth Games.

KG: Yes, but why? If Canada does not cut the ties with the monarchy and Britain, it will be impossible to exercise any kind of politics with respect to multiculturalism.

WA: The monarchy comes up from time to time but the Canadian government considers it a non-issue; there is still a lot of support for it. In my view, the monarchy is an example of false historicity; it signifies colonialism and post-colonialism, which are expressed in terms of so-called tradition, heritage, and roots. In Canada, the French and English ethnocultural groups have appropriated history unto themselves and denied it to other groups. The monarchy is a mechanism by which non-English ethnocultural groups are voided of their own historicity; not only does the monarchy imply subservience to colonial practices, it ties them to a particular language. I dispute your statement that Canada has no language; I would call it a language of submission. The post-colonial state means domination over the different. We already talked about how, during the Trudeau and Mulroney eras, the state maintained and imposed control of ethnic representations. The effect of this, in an inversion of your comments, is that ethnocultural groups themselves have found that they have a language, but no voice. Ethnic writers, critics, the go-between agents, the cultural operators have tried to re-appropriate the assimilating mechanisms through their own storytelling, but have failed. Let's look at it in terms of products of narrative: poetry, short stories, novels, theatre. By and large, writers have failed to recognize how differentiation is produced outside a multicultural state: in other words, the origins of their own difference. What they have assimilated – unconsciously, I believe – are the attitudes and beliefs of state-imposed multiculturalism. The mechanism by which representations are made has been supplied and processed through a language of dismissal. If we look at Italian-Canadian writing, we see that very few writers have been able to present an ongoing relationship between the host country

45

and the country they left. This has allowed for other things to happen: false representation mechanisms, false identity paradigms, and the possibility of the practice of post-colonial discourse from the country of origin. Looking at Canadian experience, we find ourselves in a bifurcated moment: either the assimilation into the process of state multiculturalism, which leads to total assimilation, or the recuperation of the post-colonial Italian discourse of representation, which claims that this entity, the ethno-cultural Italian-Canadian identity, belongs, in a perverted way, to the Italian experience. This bifurcation has produced mechanisms and political representations that void the Italian-Canadian voices. How is this possible? Because there is no critical ability to see through these mechanisms. Perhaps there is a marked point of distancing from this process. In the preface to Francesco Loriggio's anthology *L'Altra Storia*, Loriggio claims that the production of Italian-Canadian literary texts posits the possibility of redefining not only Italian-Canadian literature but also Italian literature itself. Now, with respect to defining Italian-Canadian literature, Italian-Canadian critics and intellectuals, especially those who were there at the moment of paradigm formations, have failed completely. I'm referring to the first meeting of the Italian-Canadian Writers' Association, which took place in 1987 in Vancouver, while a recognition of an

Italian-Canadian reality has not even happened yet. This reality is contained within the discourse of ethnocultural representations. In fact, certain Italian-Canadians have made it so that an act of self-censorship has occurred that has eliminated the possibility for other generations to come into this process and to realize their own difference. We have to boil down all discourse to the differential aspect in the dialogue, if you will, between the ghetto and the centre, the margins and centre power, as far as identity affirmations are concerned.

KG: In addition to the Italian-Canadian cultural experience, we have to keep in mind that there is a heritage program established by the Canadian state that promotes uniqueness of various ethnic communities. This apparatus is bounded by the practices of go-between agents, the mediators, the community intellectuals, the opinion leaders of the ethnic communities. This mediating process consists of two things: possessive individualism and the idea of distinctiveness of their own unique community.

WA: Or unique reality.

KG: Or unique reality. In either case – possessive individualism and distinctiveness – we experience the phenomenon of Mailer, somebody who is in the public eye and, as a result, descends into a state of narcissism and chronic infantilism, constantly gazing at himself in the figurative mirror. Such a state perpetuates the primary objective of the dominant discourse: a set of non-communicating communities with no interaction between or among intellectuals of each ethnic community. Therefore, we have again the phenomenon of divide, consume and conquer, within the boundaries of the state. Such a model is a perfect example of an established control management.

WA: If you look, then you realize why these communities are not communicating – because it is a process that denies the ability to communicate. In other words, it negates multiculturalism at the same time that it affirms it. Isn't that beautiful? You see, there is no possibility for the individualistic notion of community to penetrate the other space and to realize its common ties to a multicultural framework. The multicultural framework divides, consumes and conquers.

KG: We can observe the same thing in the academic world, where we have different communities – scientific, world communities – that produce their own forms of specialized knowledge. And they distribute their knowledge to other scientific communities, so that people outside of these communities are unaware of many developments and new knowledge.

WA: Which becomes a knowledge bounded by death, death of the passage of information, which is compartmentalized and delineated.

KG: Precisely.

WA: And what is more, these intellectual communities are grounded in and bound by time. With the passage of three, four generations, and I remind you of the Carleton University experience, the process has an ultimate end, which is a disappearing act, because in the end it must give way to the dictates of the polarized bicultural state. All these multiplicities are bounded by their own extension mechanism: chronic infantilism.

KG: If you want to examine such a model and put it into a political or social perspective, then you are seen as a danger to the system, because the system wants to keep such a model alive so that it can perpetuate its own capital. I'm talking about different kinds of systems, which, although they are different, have something in common: power.

WA: But there is the rhetorical figure that is subservient to what we are saying: the synecdoche, where the part represents the whole, or vice versa. There is a continuous displacement of the mechanism of control. We start in Canada and end up in Kosovo where we see the replication of the model on a greater scale. But this greater scale is controlled and, at the same time, it puts into practice the state-imposed multicultural paradigm and erases histories. We must try to understand what is meant by the intervention of the multi-culturalist model in terms of local histories and how these local histories . . .

KG: Perhaps original histories.

WA: Yes, how these original histories are removed and reinvested with a new meaning that presents them in a never-ending model of the present, which is chronic infantilism. The removal of history is the replication of chronic infantilism.

KG: I don't like to stay just with communities, because ethnic communities are one particular model in which the system exercises control and power relations. We have to see communities in a broader sense. We have ethnic communities, academic communities, and cultural communities. When it comes to academic communities, as I was trying to explain previously, there is something that we have to analyze in terms of isolation and lack of interaction.

WA: But we can apply the term "ethnic communi-ties" figuratively to any group that has been tar-geted and manufactured and becomes fodder for consumption in the capitalist world. I am think-ing specifically of many young people, from hip hoppers to anti-globalization protesters.

KG: We can certainly apply such a model to other groups, although we have to take into account that the symptoms of possessive individualism and chronic infantilism are not just psychological idiosyncrasies of an ethnic community, including the Anglo or French. These symptoms are political, and we have to interpret them politically. They can be observed in other settings, like universities, media and entertainment industries, corporations, and political parties. These other settings, or container spaces, are places where many voices are heard, but there are no real interactions. There are, of course, interactions when it comes to matters of business. There are joint ventures to increase the initial capital control, but when it comes to a political added value or a cultural added value, then we don't have pluralism, we don't have polyphony – we have monologues. Given this, it is not surprising that the proposed model for a working cultural model in North America and, in particular, in Canada, is not a transcultural or intercultural one, but multicultural, which means an endless process of silence and death of identity. Who can understand not just what happened in an ethnic community but also what is going on in various academic spaces in which there is no communication? One can observe a similar structure in the workings of non-governmental organizations [NGOs]. NGOs do not communicate; they do not have an integrated network to go above and beyond the politics of the state; they are not entities that can be . . .

WA: . . . That can perform on their own.

KG: Or at least they are not entities that can shake the system from the roots. They do not have an appropriate network to extend into an integrated political plan for implementation.

WA: Then what you're positing, once again, is the idea of the boundedness of the discourse. The official discourses that we hear are mechanisms of control; they supply their own prefabricated answers. The whole official discourse integrates into itself its alternative discourse. NGOs become the alternative official answer to state apparatuses, and, as such, they nullify the possibility of alternative discourses. The utopic – let's call it for what it is – the utopic desire for alternative *modus operandi* cannot come into being; the language that is used to indicate and formulate answers to social problems has already been supplied. It's a given within the official discourse that contains the alternative discourse. So that utopic is the margin that precisely defines the concrete materiality of the state. But we have already seen as a process during the twentieth century the elimination of utopic discourse as something non-essential or non-productive. To say that we live in the best of all worlds is possible because what we're given is the absolute model of existence. This has already been explained by Fukuyama. We must really confront what the end of History means in today's society. If you look around, you see manifestations of a continuous permanence of History. If you consider music, if you look at fashion or any modes of representation of so-called individuality, what you see is a conglomeration of historical representations. What were once different time intervals co-exist within the same time continuum. Now for me this is a formulation of the perfect absolute of the presence of the polyphonic within the monolithic reality of the lifeworld, as an addition by the new capitalist modes of production; that is, globalization. There is no more ability – and I'm not claiming that history entails a linearity or a progress – but it doesn't have the idea of differentiation anymore. If there is anything that we can claim about history, it is the continuous process of differentiations in terms of time. Right now, time seems to have become a collapsed category that embraces the recycling and re-enactments of differences that were claimed by His-story. In the present time, there are no more differentiations. There's only a consuming apparatus that governs all different possibilities, which have already been set and are re-represented for us, as I said, for consumption and that presents us with an eternal present. Modern Western industrialized society lives for the moment. Perhaps this is the other critical version of what Fukuyama claimed as being the end of History.

KG: Fukuyama's concept of the end of History is a perfect result of various historical developments. For example, the end of the Cold War . . .

WA: The fall of the Berlin Wall.

KG: Yes, but apart from these historical developments, we have to reconsider the role of technology and the intervention of technology into history to the point that the end of history comes as a matter of the end of time and the end of space. In our time, we enter the realm of spiritual reality; that is, the new age, and the presence of technology saturates our sense of history – time stands still. The only thing that the intellectuals can do is to use these technologies in order to be part of the cult of culture. They just consume the . . .

WA: . . . The given materiality of the world.

KG: Of the world, of technology, and, because of such poverty, I would say, they go outside to marginal developments in order to appropriate their discourses, bring them back into their discourse, but in such a way that they can be totally capitalized and, with no dangerous consequences, neutralized, to a point that these marginal groups are no longer a threat to the survival of the power system.

WA: So what you are doing is denouncing precisely how authenticity is removed from the lifeworld.

KG: Yes. At the same time, I'm trying to say that the concepts of time and space are a perfect result of the existing model of technological society.

WA: Look at the dates. In 1989, we hear about the end of History in an article by Fukuyama. According to him, the 1990s were to be a decade free of ideological wars. But it actually produced two major world wars: the Gulf War and Kosovo, which saw the internationalization of local conflict and the application of post-modern technologies to modern warfare, like the so-called "smart bomb." There is continuous tension that is represented as a means of control. What Fukuyama envisioned as the end of conflict actually becomes officially administered conflict.

KG: But conflicts must be controlled in order for political power system to survive. And political power systems have their own means to prevent an absolute state of catastrophe. Catastrophe must be controlled, it must have boundaries, but, importantly, it must be exported. The political power system, particularly the Anglo-American, must be protected by critical masses who can impose the "peace process" of the state. You remember what happened in the U.S.A. in the 1960s? Many people, for example, know about the assassination of Martin Luther King – the Ku Klux Klan, in collaboration with other authoritarian agencies in the U.S.A., killed him. But what about Malcolm X, who wanted a separate state for blacks within the U.S.A.? He was assassinated, too. Many people have no idea about Malcolm X's struggle against the white power system in America. Political power systems try to mask the forms of oppression . . .

WA: . . . And resistance.

KG: And catastrophes. That's why most Americans think that the U.S.A. won the war in Vietnam. They base their opinions on Hollywood movies. We are seeing not just the end of history, but the masking of history, and this masking is possible thanks to media and entertainment industries and technology, which can be efficiently applied to the point that history is erased, or at least masked according to the interests of the power system.

WA: An example of a collapsing mechanism like the one you're describing would be the rehabilitation, in the course of a decade, of the Mulroney government. We have gone from removing him from government and the reduction of the Progressive Conservative Party to two members in Parliament, to the rehabilitation of the Mulroney era as one of good times and prosperity. In the space of one decade, his image rose, fell and then was resurrected again. Much the same thing happened in Quebec with the Henri Bourassa government. What we have is a speeded-up process of denunciation and recuperation in our postmodern world. Many public figures, like Nixon in the U.S.A., have gone through a process of analysis and criticism of their mechanisms of control and their trampling of democratic processes to being resurrected as great men who helped their country. So we can erase historicity from history.

KG: It's quite interesting to see the way that history is erased, not just in terms of a scientific discipline or as a literary text, but even in art and public representations of historical events. For example, if you visit Ottawa, Montreal or Toronto, you will never see a statue showing the indigenous peoples' struggle against the colonizers. What we have is – and now I will use this term – a totalitarian discourse, which can be found in all levels of society and culture. A newcomer to Canada will never understand, will never be exposed to . . .

WA: . . . Will never see the reality of Canada.

KG: Precisely. This kind of reality is erased from the physical landscape.

WA: This point is emphasized by representations of statehood in national museums and other buildings. Let's make a comparison between the Muse-

um of Civilization and the National Gallery in
Ottawa.

KG: Those are both empty buildings. With respect to
the Museum of Civilization, first of all, the power
system devoted sections to the Indians or to the
Inuit people, but only in such a way that history is
depicted according to consumable precepts and
superficial representations. And then there is the
elimination of ethnic struggle between Anglo and
Franco. I mean, there is a lack of not just appreciation of history but of political sensitivity. There is
a lack of consciousness of historicity. Aesthetically,
the National Gallery is an authoritarian building
that resembles fascist architecture in the era of
Hitler and Mussolini. That's quite strange,
because it was designed by Moshe Safdie.[24]

WA: Perhaps it's a question of having internalized
and masked the process of oppression and repack-
aged it as a mechanism of representation.

KG: I think this happened there, and that's why it's
so ugly. If you actually go in and look at the
exhibits, you again see the dominant discourse at
work. The National Gallery is an authoritarian,
almost fascist, building outside and inside, but
architecturally speaking, the Canadian Museum
of Civilization, designed by an aboriginal, Douglas Cardinal, is rather nice.[25]

WA: But look at the way the National Gallery, even

symbolically, re-appropriates light. I mean, light is contained within, light which is supposed to reflect naturally on the various artistic representations, but really, if you look at it, the whole building is like a religious installation. It's a beautiful "natural process" of the containment of light, which gives perspective to the artificial representations of reality. So it's a mechanism within a mechanism of control. Within the cathedral, there is already the idea of the surplus spiritual waste of capitalist society.

KG: Yes, but this is a controlled representation of control that must be seen as political. Otherwise, we will have only an abstract, vague idea about living in Canada.

WA: What about the locations of these buildings?

KG: Yes, just opposite the federal Parliament.

WA: And the American Embassy. Why is this? Clearly, it's been decided that these sites all have some interest in each other.

KG: It's also close to the French and British Embassies. So there's a kind of force field that covers the American Embassy, the Parliament of Canada, the Museum of Civilization, the National Gallery plus the other two embassies, the French and British, giving a perfect indication of post-modernism in a post-colonial world. Someone trying to discover what Canada is all about has to go back to the notion of the panopticon developed by Foucault,[26] where at least we have to deconstruct the post-colonial meaning or social settings or container spaces in order to re-write history above and beyond biculturalism or multiculturalism. Of course, the big question will be, who's going to write such a history? Not the intellectuals of the power system or the go-between mediators or agents of such a system, working within communities. Re-writing history must be done according to the politics of interaction, in terms of the politics of authenticity.

WA: And of tension.

KG: Definitely. Canada must be declared a non-monarchist state, unconnected to the politics of London, Washington, and Paris.

WA: The retention of the monarchy is part of a materiality of dominance, insofar as the monarchist discourse ties itself to other visible representations of the official dominant minority discourses. I think we have to continually repeat that the Anglophone and Francophone communities are minorities. And other iconic or material representations of dominance, such as the Museum of Civilization and the National Gallery, are conducive to a singular discourse, of something that seems to represent variety but in reality reduces variety down to one official representation. At the same time that it represents, it denies – as with any iconic symbol. But then what we have to ask is: precisely what is being denied? I mean, we have to differentiate and reposition ourselves within official representations to see precisely what is being denied. Not just marginalized, but denied. Erased from history.

KG: Current representations or presentations of history are a part of the Canadian biculturally driven structure, incorporated into a self-indulgent society that sees history as entertainment; this attitude is reinforced by marketing. Such a development leads to a deceptive narrative, what I call a "Pinocchio narrative," in which the state and its own cultural agencies use ethnicity at the same time that they deny it, leading to, as you said, cultural genocide. Further, the groovy family narrative of the Canadian state uses biculturalism in almost a seductive way to sensationalize Anglo-French constitutional confrontation. The outcome of such a process in a Pinocchio society is based on falsification, as well as on combination of technological wizardry and computer-generated imagery. In such an artificial society, we must seek to discover what is really behind the dark reflective glasses of Canadian culture. There is a saying in Greece that God said to us, "Think alone." This thinking requires the cultivation of something special. In Greece we call it *paideia,* which means education but implies something more than that: knowledge, learning.

WA: When you talk about the technology and the shaping of the structures of modern technology I presume that you are referring to the World Wide Web, the Internet, and also to the possibility of interconnectivity with other systems. We must reiterate that, although the Internet seems to provide an anarchical representation of various interests and groups from all over the world, and seems to allow for the promulgation of diverse kinds of information to many people, in the end, it becomes a beautiful trap. And this trap is also a mechanism of control. There are lots of places where the control can be established. Let's not forget that the source of every e-mail message is known, that viruses and worms can attack all of us, and that every site that a person visits can be traced. Hence the trap. Hence the possibility for the Net to provide a forum for conflict and antagonism. Furthermore, as computer use increases, more and more people become dependent on computers for their livelihood. We are helpless without it, slaves to it. And as more and more people start to work at home or use the Net for every kind of social interaction from shopping to chat lines to finding lovers, the Net becomes a form of artificial society, a false community based on its own means of repression. The moment that it comes into being, it is easily identifiable as a source of antagonism within the perfect system, which means that a virus can be eliminated from our own linguistic possibilities if, to quote the avante-garde performance artist and musician Laurie Anderson, "language is a virus."

KG: And then there is a linguistic domination due to almost exclusive use of . . .

WA: . . .The English language.

KG: Yes. Not to mention the flood of various kinds of useless information.

WA: That's right. There is not enough time to verify or to ascertain anything, so this overabundance leads to a state of paralysis, where everything collapses onto itself and becomes nil, the void. So, apart from the fact that it's a mechanism of control, it is also the erasure of knowledge, the trivialization of information.

KG: Although apart from the phenomenon of linguistic colonialism that we experience through the use of the Net, there is another point related to the notion of information. In order to get the information on the Net, people must know how to use it. And not just that, they must know enough to ask appropriate questions.

WA: It's a knowledge that encodes the interconnectivity into a precise mechanism of representation, which means that this encoding is also, in a manner of speaking, ossified. In other words, the system imposes the use of English, with the result that English becomes a code not just reducing down to the bone, but really structuring to a rigid mechanism or a rigid skeleton. This, once again, denies precisely what it tries to achieve, which is the ability to communicate freely, independent of any mechanism of control. Can we call it a necessary illusion? This is where Bissoondath went wrong, because this really is what his book should have been about – the necessary illusion of communication.

KG: People who use the Net believe that it breaks down hierarchy. But this is an illusion, because in order to get the information you must know exactly how to use the Net, and even if you know this, you have to deal with various mediators. There are various levels of mediation. Therefore, hierarchy is not broken down; instead, we see the undeniable presence of hierarchy in the Internet.

WA: The hierarchy of the lifeworld is reflected in the virtual world.

KG: Yes. And there's another illusion that we have to mention – the illusion that we're moving to a global world and, in particular, to a global public space. The notion of global public space is reinforced by cultural agencies or cultural mediators and programmed intellectuals, who play a role by bringing up the discourse of post-colonialism.

WA: Let's go back to what we said earlier: knowledge is power; power is control. You cannot escape from this interconnectivity. It is interesting, then, to note that whenever certain discourses are enunciated and become public, we lose the perspective of the origin of those discourses. It's the ability of terms such as "new world order," "post-colonialism," "globalization," "access," and "transparency" – a belated *glasnost* and *perestroika* – to mask the originator and point of origin that we should note. At the same time, they mask the sources of power so that it seems that the individual appropriates power. But in this appropriation, the individual also renounces the so-called private sphere where he or she is able to react and formulate a critical analysis of the world. The dominance of the public sphere is really the erasure of individuality. I am not talking about individuality in a narcissistic practice à la Michael Jackson and the Me generation of the 1980s, but rather individuality as the formative process of a democratic reality and of a democratic lifeworld.

KG: Or citizenship.

WA: Or citizenship. Precisely.

KG: We must keep in mind that the Internet is a

product of a scientific–military conglomeration – it was invented by the Pentagon, after all – and now we still are witnessing such a connection, not just in the form of the Internet, but in various areas of public life. Although such a connection, a scientific or academic connection with military . . .

WA: . . . And with research apparatuses?

KG: Yes. These are channelled by cultural and media interests that create a new type of ideology: an ideology of technology. Such an ideology creates a kind of three-ring circus. These three rings are, first of all, a distortion, but not in the artistic form of abstract expressionism the way that Bacon distorted the body or the face.[27] I mean societal or cultural distortion. The second ring is the legitimization of the anomalies of the power elite system. And the third ring represents the integration of the ethnic "minorities" into the legitimization process.

WA: I am reminded of an Italian-Canadian painter, Nick Palazzo, who died some years ago, and who, in his representation of disease – AIDS – configured and represented precisely this transparency of the body, meaning that the body becomes a collapsed system of representation and at the same time appears as an unveiled reality that has no ground in concrete reality anymore. The body is immaterial.[28]

KG: What strikes me right now, particularly in this epoch, is that we experience and believe in the way military technology becomes part of the cultural apparatus, and such an apparatus gives us ways of dreaming. It gives us ways of administering thinking to the point that we don't even understand that we are slaves or prisoners of our own systems. We think that we are free to choose and to consume . . .

WA: In the best of all possible worlds, because this is the end point of everything that we analyze and criticize.

KG: Most intellectuals think that technologies are scientific, although they are not; they are political. It's not accidental that there is a kind of ideological discourse that separates politics from economy, politics from culture, politics from life, and leaves politics to the politicians. But we have to understand that we live in a society that separates everything to the point that we're now entering the era of transhumanism, which is a movement that wants to separate mind from body.[29] So all these kinds of things, coming from particular dominant ideological points of reference or view, must be exposed in order to show that the depths of a control mechanism or control management that . . .

WA: . . . Is death bound. One thing – something that I thought of when you were talking about the role of

the military research and industrial complexes –
why is no connection made between so-called post-
modernism and this other entity, reality. I mean, it
seems to me that the post-modernist discourse has
been created in order to undo other realities. Post-
modernism says that there are no more great ide-
ologies; everything is a minimal ideology, and
therefore what triumphs is a sort of an individualistic reality. Well, what we are doing is precisely
deconstructing the post-modern discourse and
going to the origins of these types of discourses to
see their effect on the lifeworld. Because by invest-
ing meaning within the post-modernist discourse,
you get a diminishment of individual reality, and
this diminishment is connected, once again, to a
system of management control.

KG: And this management control is quite obvious
not just in the North American society, but everywhere in the world right now. However, it does
take place in various levels. For example, Bill
Clinton brought many experts to the White
House to talk about the challenge facing children
in America. They talked about school violence
and early childhood development education and
social security. This is telling. The U.S. president
and all his experts like to control – quite correctly
– the violence in schools, yet at the same time, the
United States exercises violent politics everywhere in the world in the name of . . .

WA: . . . Just causes and higher values. Humanitarian reasons?

KG: Yes, but in a selective way.

WA: I think that violence in schools is a part of the American model of life and is actually a form of resistance, perhaps an irrational one, to domination. The problem is that there is no possibility of recuperating it or its leading to critical discourses and actions against the oppression of transnational capitalism.

KG: I think that what they produce is a transhumanist kind of state, because everything is based on separations. And if you separate everything, then, of course, you get back to the British axiom of divide, consume and conquer. This is what we live . . .

WA: And are freely allowed and even encouraged to exercise in our day-to-day lives.

KG: Still, you can only accumulate so much power. I think that we are soon going to experience an entropic finality. Reification and depoliticized speech by intellectuals, writers and artists. We experience the aestheticization of politics and the "abuse of forms," as Metaxas pointed out. What do you think?

WA: I think that's an accurate forecast for the new millennium, but we must not renounce positivity.

We must not succumb to a critical reading that inspires only passivity. If anything, what we have shown, criticized and talked about reveals the bounded reality that is part of the system of oppression as well. This system, this hyperstructure, cannot continue *ad infinitum*.

KG: But we cannot wait for this to happen. We need an active praxis.

WA: Which is to bring about a critical mass that will collapse the system before more destruction, misery, and horrors occur.

KG: So, if I take into account all that we have said in our conversation, my question to you is, where are you from, William?

WA: From nowhere but I am on a trajectory that has been directed by what we said today.

NOTES

1   Canada began and adopted an official multiculturalism policy in 1971 during the Liberal prime ministry of Pierre Trudeau. In 1986, under the Progressive Conservative government of Brian Mulroney, the Government of Canada passed the *Employment Equity Act* and, in 1988, the *Canadian Multiculturalism Act*. According to the federal government, "The Multiculturalism Policy affirms that Canada recognizes and values its rich ethnic and racial diversity. The *Canadian Multiculturalism Act* gives specific direction to the federal government to work toward achieving equality in the economic, social, cultural and political life of the country. Through its multiculturalism policy, the Government of Canada aims to help build a more inclusive society based on respect, equality and the full participation of all citizens, regardless of race, ethnic origin, language or religion."
    < http://www.infocan.gc.ca/facts/multi_e.html >
    Sounds great in theory, but the authors will contend that there is a great gulf between the theory and practice of multiculturalism in Canada.

2   The Multicultural Program is administered under the aegis of the Department of Canadian Heritage. The minister of this department at the time of this writing was Sheila Copps. The Secretary of State for Multiculturalism was Hedy Fry.

3   According to the 1991 federal census, the most recent for which figures are available, 28% of the Canadian population reported British origin; 23% French; 15.4% other European; and 6% Asian, Arabic or African. Further, the census noted that the immigrant population represented 16% of the entire population; the proportion of immigrants from Europe was 54%;

the proportion from Asia was 25%.
<http://www.hc-sc.gc.ca/datahpsb/npu/cpc5.htm>

4   In an article published in the *National Post* (Saturday, April 10, 1999), Scott Reid quotes Atwood as claiming that she had excluded immigrant authors from consideration because it seemed "dangerous to talk about *Canadian* patterns of sensibility in the work of people who entered and/or entered-and-left the country at a developmentally late stage of their lives." Scott characterized this attitude as monolithic and homogeneous and noted that Atwood's *Survival* has ". . . no room for individualists, dissenters or the purveyors of impurities from overseas . . ."

5   From the introduction to Davies's 1994 work *Hunting Stuart & The Voice of the People*: "In a government like ours, the Crown is the abiding and unshakeable element in government. Politicians may come and go, but the Crown remains and certain aspects of our system pertain to it which are not dependent on any political party. In this sense the Crown is the consecrated spirit of Canada."

6   Conrad Black, chairman of Hollinger Inc., created the *National Post* in October of 1998. About a year after this duologue took place, Black sold half of the *Post* and most of Hollinger's Canadian newspapers and its Internet properties to CanWest Global Communications Corp. for about $3.2 billion. This purchase was the largest transaction in the history of the Canadian media industry and effectively made CanWest the largest daily newspaper publisher in Canada as well as the country's leading international multimedia news, information and entertainment company. As of July, 2001, CanWest owned 14 major, English-language metropolitan dailies, including the *Ottawa Citizen*, *Calgary Herald*, *Edmonton Journal*.

7 German mathematician Gottfried Wilhelm Leibnitz (1646–1716), concurrent with but independent of Sir Isaac Newton, developed the branch of mathematics known as calculus. Leibnitz was also a philosopher. In his *The Monadology* of 1714, he argued that all things consist of uncountable units called monads. Each monad's unique properties determined each thing's past, present and future. Monads acted predictably; the corollary of this is that Christian faith and science do not necessarily have to be in conflict and that this is "the best of all possible worlds." Voltaire satirized this philosophy in *Candide* (1759), which, inspired by the devastating Lisbon earthquake of 1755, shows the absurdity and inhumanity of this idea.

8 *Dead Man* is the story of a young man named William Blake who travels far into the American West during the latter part of the nineteenth century, where he meets an outcast Indian named "Nobody." Nobody thinks that the young man is the reincarnation of the poet William Blake. Circumstances turn Blake into an outlaw. "Thrown into a world that is cruel and chaotic, his eyes are opened to the fragility that defines the realm of the living. It is as though he passes through the surface of a mirror, and emerges into a previously unknown world on the other side."

9 Cornelius Castoriadis (1922-1997) was a political thinker, social critic, psychoanalyst, and a Sovietologist. Born in Constantinople in 1922, the Castoriadis family moved that same year to Greece to avoid Greco-Turkish strife. As a young man, he become involved with a Trotskyist faction of the Greek Communist Party. Castoriadis was known for his political insight and was particularly prescient in his assessment of the Communist Party's attempted coup d'état in 1944, which, instead of propelling Greece toward a classless society, instead gave rise to a totalitarian

regime similar to Russia's, much as he had predicted. Castoriadis eventually moved to France, where he joined the Trotskyists and began to develop his form of radical anti-Stalinism. He opposed the Fourth International, which was advocating an unconditional defense of the U.S.S.R., and at about this time, co-founded the revolutionary journal and group *Socialisme ou Barbarie* (1948-1967). *Socialisme ou Barbarie* provided a radical critique of communism based upon the idea of workers' management and was influential in the Paris student–worker rebellion of 1968. In his later writings, Castoriadis examined the co-birth of philosophy and politics in ancient Greece, paying particular attention to the rise of citizen democracy in fifth century Athens. He contrasted this development with today's so-called democracies, in which representative institutions of governance establish permanent place holders divorced from the average citizen. He used the term *liberal oligarchy* to describe Western political arrangments. Castoriadis spent the last thirty years of his life developing his original concept of history as an imaginary creation, not subject to rational, natural or divine planning or edicts. He believed that there was no inevitable dialectical process and no reason in History. (See the following note on Francis Fukuyama for a very different point of view of history.)

10 In the summer of 1989, Francis Fukuyama, a deputy director of the U.S. State Department's Policy Planning Staff, published an article entitled "The End of History?" in *The National Interest,* a quarterly political magazine published in Washington, DC. The article was an international sensation, eliciting both praise and denunciation. In the article, which was followed by a 1992 book entitled *The End of History and the Last Man*, Fukuyama argued that liberal democracy, that is, American-style capitalism, constituted the end point of all ideological evolution and was the "final

form of human government." As such, we have wit-
nessed the end of History. Note the use of the upper-
case H. Fukuyama meant to distinguish history, the
course of normal events, from History writ large,
which he defined as "a single, coherent, evolutionary
process." He contended that earlier forms of human
government were irrational and fraught with internal
contradictions and strife; their demise was inevitable.
He further contended that liberal democracy, meaning,
of course, the American form of governance, was free
from internal contradictions that brought about the
fall of the Communist bloc, and therefore had proved
itself the superior, and inevitable, form of government.
With the attack on NYC's World Trade Centre, which
occurred shortly before the publication of this book,
Fukuyama's claims appear even more tenuous.

11 Olive Coalition is the name given to the coalition of
centre- and left-leaning parties in Italy that was founded in May of 1996 under the leadership of Romano
Prodi. Major branches of the Olive Coalition included
the Democratic Party of the Left, a spin-off from the
extinct Communist Party, led by Massimo D'Alema,
and the Communist Refoundation, led by Fausto
Bertinotti. D'Alema succeeded Prodi and became
leader in 1999. In May of 2000, D'Alema resigned
after the negative results in regional elections, during
which the right-wing coalition Casa della Libertà
(House of Liberty), led by media tycoon Silvio Berlusconi, won eight of 15 regions. A week after D'Alema's
resignation, the Olive Coalition appointed Giuliano
Amato to lead the new government; he was followed
by Francesco Rutelli in October of 2000. In May of
2001, the Olive Coalition was defeated by Berlusconi's
Forza Italia ("Go, Italy," the national football battle
cry) and the Casa della Libertà coalition. Two of
Berlusconi's major allies are the Alleanza Nazionale
(National Alliance, derived from the Italian Social

Movement, a direct descendent of the Republic of Salò and the fascist government after the 1943 armistice) and the Lega (Northern Separatist League, whose main contribution to Italian culture has been the green-shirted Guardia Nazionale Padana, groups with the same *esprit de corps* as Mussolini's Black Shirts). The Northern League, led by Umberto Bossi, whom some have compared to Austrian politician Jorg Haider for his attacks on the "cultural baggage" of immigrants, no longer seeks a separate state in northern Italy (that was to be called "Padania") but Bossi, along with others in the coalition, is known as a devolutionist. Berlusconi, who once worked as a singer on a cruise ship, has been in and out of court for years over tax fraud and corruption charges. Nevertheless, at the time of this writing, he was Italy's richest man; in 1999, he declared an income of 16.2 billion lira ($7.4 million), while his personal wealth was estimated by Forbes at $12.8 million. The Berlusconi family empire is huge and ranges from telecommunications to insurance to construction. It includes Fininvest, a company that controls the three commercial television stations belonging to Mediaset, Italy's major private network; the football team AC Milan; Mondadori, Italy's largest publishing house; the Mediolanum bank; a major newspaper, *Il Giornale*; and the news magazine *Panorama*.
<http://europe.cnn.com/SPECIALS/2001/italy/stories/berlusconi/>

12 Herbert Marcuse (1898-1979) was a German philosopher, who was a refugee from Hitler's Germany. He moved to the U.S. in 1934 and become professor at the University of California at San Diego in 1965. Marcuse combined theories of Marxism and Freudianism to influence radical thought in the 1960s. With the 1964 publication of *One Dimensional Man*. Marcuse posited his belief that, though modern industrial society has satisfied our material needs, it has at the same time

ignored intrinsic needs and restricted freedom. Marcuse dismissed the surface liberty of many societies as "repressive tolerance." There was no way, according to Marcuse, that a truly liberated person could ever come to terms with capitalism. As an interesting aside, in 1968 at the University of California at San Diego, Marcuse taught Angela Davis, of Black Panther fame.

13 Antonio Gramsci (1891-1937), founder of the Italian Communist party, was imprisoned by Mussolini's fascists when they banned the Communist Party in 1926. While orthodox Marxism explained nearly everything according to economics, Gramsci added the crucial cultural dimension. He showed how, once a state enforces ideological authority, or cultural hegemony, it no longer needs to use violence to control the populace. In other words, defining and controlling culture is vital; once you get into people's heads, you control their hearts, thoughts, wallets, and their fates. Gramsci's philosophy of praxis calls for organizations to replace capitalism. In developing this thought, he refined his theory of intellectuals as organizers, as activists rather than ideologues. For Gramsci, capitalism separates the intellectual from society and creates a system in which those who know are pitted against those who don't. He wrote of the intellectual as organizer of a revolutionary practice in which the revolution is carried out by self-conscious men.

14 Michel de Montaigne (1533-1592) is credited with the development of the personal essay. Noted for his wit and intellect, deep knowledge of classical literature and abiding humanism, Montaigne mistrusted the pretensions and presumptions of philosophy. If his writings contain more allusions and anecdotes than formal arguments, they are nevertheless cogent and full of insight. Though he maintained that faith and divine revelation were necessary to counter the limitations of

human reason, his writings laid the ground upon which rationalists (for example, Descartes) built their theories that knowledge is independent of the senses.

15 Many companies and organizations seek to spread their influence by financing university chairs and departments. In the United States, foundations like Coors Brewing and Olin, a petrochemical and munitions company, have spent millions in some of America's Ivy League universities to spread the great news about private enterprise. An article by Susan George published in *Dissent* magazine supplies the following telling anecdote.

<http://victoria.ca/uq/sgeorge.html>

In 1988, Allan Bloom, author of *The Closing of the American Mind* and director of the University of Chicago's Olin Centre for Inquiry into the Theory and Practice of Democracy (a $3.6 million Olin grant), invited a State Department official to speak. This official wrote an article proclaiming the end of ideology and the triumph of Western neo-liberal values. The paper was published in the *National Interest* (a $1 million Olin subsidy) and edited by Irving Kristol (Olin Distinguished Professor at New York University Graduate School of Business). Kristol then published responses to the paper by himself, Bloom, and Samuel Huntington (of the Olin Institute for Strategic Studies at Harvard.) This manufactured and orchestrated debate was then picked up by the *New York Times*, the *Washington Post* and *Time Magazine*. The rest is history, well, the End of History, by Francis Fukuyama (see note 10 above).

16 Located in Vancouver, the Fraser Institute was founded in 1974. Its Website notes that the purpose of the Institute is "to redirect public attention to the role markets can play in providing for the economic and social well-being of Canadians . . . the Fraser Institute

has consistently led the intellectual consensus on key public policy . . . The Institute's program continues to have an impact in stretching the frontiers of the Canadian public policy debate. In areas such as welfare reform, privatization, taxation, free trade, government debt, education, poverty, deregulation, health care, labour markets, economic restructuring and the role of government – the fresh, innovative ideas about market solutions to economic problems come from The Fraser Institute." Many others take a much harsher view of the role of the Fraser Institute in affecting Canadian public policy. Environmentalists characterize it as "harshly anti-environmental," those working in human services decry its hard-hearted attitude towards poverty, and teachers' associations across the country are at loggerheads with its lionization of rigid testing, private school funding and support for the marketization of schools. There are many similar ideological think tanks that support so-called neo-liberal thought in the West. Among the major American ones are the American Enterprise Institute, the Heritage Foundation (associated with Ronald Reagan), the Hoover Institution on War Revolution and Peace (dedicated to the study of communism and the Cold War), the Cato Institute, the Manhattan Institute for Policy Research (founded by once CIA head William Casey), whose mission is to critique U.S. government income-distribution programs. Abroad, London is the home of the Centre for Policy Studies and the Adam Smith Institute, a major proponent of privatization and advisor on this issue to the World Bank. The Swiss Alps are a backdrop for the mysterious Mount Pelerin Society, which first brought American and European conservatives together in 1947. Membership is by invitation only and member names are not advertised, though it is known that Margaret Thatcher belongs and Milton Friedman is a fan.

17 Diane Francis, "Immigration Sponsorship Policy a Disaster." The *Edmonton Journal*, March 14, 1999.

18 In November of 1975, French President Giscard d'Estaing convened an economic summit of major industrialized countries – France, Germany, Britain, Japan and the United States – intended to establish an informal forum to discuss world economic issues. This original Group of Five was joined in 1976-77 by Italy and Canada and became the Group of Seven (G-7). In the 1980s the meetings became more formalized, and full media coverage became standard. As well, the G-7 agenda became broader with the arrival of new leaders (Reagan, Mitterand, Kohl, Thatcher), who were keen to bring a political element to the talks. For example, at the 1983 Williamsburg Summit in the U.S., the G-7 agreed to support the deployment of U.S. Pershing and Cruise missiles to Europe to confront Soviet SS20 missiles. The end of the Cold War and the rise of globalization have brought about further changes. During the early 1990s, the G-7 leaders were involved in the Uruguay Round of GATT negotiations, which gave birth to the World Trade Organization (WTO), and Russia became a member, necessitating a name change to G-8. The G-8 has come under great scrutiny and criticism based on the belief by many that it is an elitist organization that has no empathy for poor countries and that it is out to promote a global corporatist agenda. At the July 2001 G-8 meeting in Genoa, Italy, protests became violent, one protester was shot and killed by the police, and hundreds were injured. Shortly after the mayhem ended, Canadian Prime Minister Jean Chrétien announced that next year's meeting would be held in the idyllic, remote – and bear-infested – region of Kananaskis, Alberta.

19 Literally, *realism*, a nineteenth-century Italian literary and artistic movement inspired by the naturalism of

Zola, it proposes a rigorous faith to representation of people, places, and circumstances. Its subjects tend to be people of humble circumstances who must fight to survive.

20 Giambattista Vico (1668-1744), professor of rhetoric at the University of Naples from 1699, is considered by many to be one of Italy's greatest philosophers. Vico posited the principle that whatever is true *(verum)* and whatever is made *(factum)* are convertible – we can only be sure of something if we have created it. Attempting to imitate nature through experiments yields only approximate truths, whereas, because societies are our own creations, the human sciences can offer exact knowledge. In his *The New Science* of 1725, Vico used this thesis to develop a philosophy of history that anticipated many of the central tenets of nineteenth-century historicism. He argued that historical events parallel the growth of the individual, from infancy through to maturity, old age and death. That is, history follows a cyclical pattern of *corsi e ricorsi* in which cultural, intellectual, economic, linguistic, and political developments are all related. For Vico, the evolving needs and interests of individuals determined social change.

21 While it is true that opposition to the Kosovo war in Canada seemed muted, there were protests on the part of ethnic communities. I remember in particular one such protest/rally in Edmonton held by the local Serbian community, and I am sure that there were others. Although the protest did get coverage in the local Edmonton media, perhaps the issue is not so much that groups were silent, but that the mainstream media give only passing coverage to non-mainstream points of view.

22 While the exact quantity of bombs dropped on Kosovo is not easily determined, there is no doubt that deplet-

ed uranium bombs were dropped not just in Kosovo but also in Iraq. Depleted uranium (DU) bombs, first used in the Gulf War, are made from the waste of enriched uranium for light water reactor fuel and nuclear warheads. Depleted uranium provides cheap material for munitions production and is economical for the nuclear industry because it reduces long-term storage costs. Serious health problems are associated with DU, including various cancers, birth defects, and kidney and respiratory problems. Upon impact DU produces a toxic radioactive dust that is carried by wind to farmers' fields. This dust is also small enough to be inhaled. Many groups have vociferously condemned the use of DU weapons. According to the Sierra Club, "[The] environmental consequences of DU weapon residue will be felt for thousands of years as its decay products continually transform into other hazardous radioactive substances in the uranium decay chain." The International Institute of Concern for Public Health in Toronto condemned the use of DU weapons, calling for a universal denunciation: "It is imperative that we denounce this radiation and toxic chemical warfare. It has been used by the U.S. and Britain against Iraq and Bosnia. It is now being used in Kosovo. It has been condemned by the U.N. Human Rights Tribunal." In addition to DU weapons, the so-called smart bombs dropped on Kosovo should have been sent to the back of the class. According to an AFP report based on confidential British Ministry of Defence documents, ". . . as many as 31 percent of the controversial cluster bombs, blamed for large numbers of civilian casualties, also missed, while laser-guided 'smart bombs' achieved only a 66-percent strike rate . . . The findings indicate that 'collateral damage' – civilian casualties and damage to property – might have been worse than previously thought."
<http://www.computec-int.com/bsc/war/archives/09-04-12.htm>

And if the lack of concern for populations in other countries isn't enough, the U.S.A. faces accusations that it does not care about its own soldiers. A 1999 report from the *San Francisco Examiner* states that the Pentagon confirmed that its jets are firing radioactive bullets in Yugoslavia. Paul Sullivan, executive director of the National Gulf War Resource Center, a coalition of groups fighting for medical care for ailing Gulf War veterans, is quoted as saying, "It's our impression that the Pentagon is not training soldiers about depleted uranium exposure . . . Our troops are not prepared."
<http://prop1.org/nucnews?9905nn/990511nn.90.htm>

For an interesting, and frightening, discussion of Gulf War Syndrome, depleted uranium and the dangers of radiation, see an article on the Canadian Coalition for Nuclear Responsibility Website, written by Dr. Rosalie Bertell, President of the International Institute of Concern for Public Health (IICPH), and Editor in Chief of International Perspectives in Public Health.
<http://ccnr.org/bertell_book.html>

23 The trade embargo on Iraq, first imposed August 6, 1990, has caused immense suffering in that country. Reports from various agencies, among them the United Nations International Children's Emergency Fund (UNICEF), estimate civilian casualties, most of them children, at over 1 million. Dr. Richard Garfield, a Columbia University professor who studies the humanitarian impact of sanctions, was quoted in a recent news release as saying, "We have good reason to believe that over 600,000 civilians have died in Iraq; that's 600,000 excess deaths caused by sanctions and war damage." A wide range of international human rights and health organizations, including the Red Cross, Amnesty International and the British Medical Association, have also denounced the humanitarian impact of the U.N. embargo.

<http://dawaparty.freeyellow.com/news/newsarchive.
html#55>

24 Moshe Safdie (born 1938 in Haifa, Israel). Educated at
McGill University in Montreal, Safdie designed Habi-
tat for Expo 67 as his student thesis. In 1984, he
designed the National Gallery of Canada. Safdie has
written extensively and has taught in Canada and in
Israel. From 1978–1984, he was the director of the
Urban Design program at Harvard, and from
1984–89, was a professor of architecture and urban
design at Harvard's Graduate School of Design. He
currently has a private practice in Boston.

25 Born in Calgary, Alberta, in 1934, Douglas J. Cardinal
was the first in a Metis family of eight children. He
studied at the University of British Columbia School of
Architecture and the University of Texas, Austin, grad-
uating in 1963 with a Bachelor of Architecture (Hon-
ours). Cardinal then returned to Alberta, where he
designed the critically acclaimed St. Mary's Roman
Catholic Church in Red Deer. Cardinal went on to
design the Grande Prairie Regional College and the St.
Albert Civic and Cultural Centre. In 1989, he collabo-
rated with Michel Languedoc to design the Canadian
Museum of Civilization. In 1992, he was awarded the
Canada Council Molson Prize for the Arts and, in
1993, was commissioned to design the Smithsonian
Institution's National Museum of the American Indian
in Washington, D.C.

26 The *panopticon* was a nineteenth century prison
design, proposed by English philosopher Jeremy Ben-
tham, where people knew they were being watched at
all times. The design was meant to apply to all kinds of
institutions, from asylums to factories. People were to
be kept in rings of individual cells, all of which could
be seen from a central observation tower. This con-

stant observation was meant to pressure them to obey the institution's rules at all times. French philosopher and intellectual Michel Foucault used the panopticon as a metaphor to describe the modern-day disciplinary power apparatus, which is based on isolation and supervision, and how people internalize social discipline, because they feel they are always being watched and, therefore, must behave properly to avoid punishment.

27 Expressionist painter Francis Bacon (1909-1992) was noted for his representations of distorted and unsettling human forms, for which, by the 1950s, he had achieved an international reputation. In defiance of convention, Bacon deliberately used the triptych format of Renaissance altarpieces to show the evils and corruption of humanity rather than the virtues of Christ. One of his best known works, "Pope Innocent X," is a reworking of a portrait by Velasquez, which Bacon made into a representation of angst.

28 Painter Nick Palazzo's brief life (1961-1991) is celebrated and chronicled in Essay Series 38, *Painting Moments: Arts, Aids and Nick Palazzo*, edited by Montreal writer Mary Melfi, published by Guernica. The book includes sixteen colour plates of the artist's work.

29 Transhumanism is a recent, fringe philosophical movement that sees the physical body as a transitory stage in the evolution of intelligence. Transhumanists advocate the use of science to move from a human to a transhuman or post-human state. Some transhumanism advocates believe that, one day, we will be able to upload human intelligence and consciousness into a computer, in effect causing the end of death.

BIBLIOGRAPHY

Atwood, Margaret. *Survival: A Thematic Guide to Canadian Literature*. Toronto: Anansi, 1972.

Anselmi, William and Kosta Gouliamos (eds.). *Mediating Culture: The Politics of Representation*. Toronto, On: Guernica, 1994.

——. *Elusive Margins: Consuming Media, Ethnicity and Culture*. Toronto, On: Guernica, 1998.

Bissoondath, Neil. *Selling Illusions: The Cult of Multiculturalism in Canada*. Toronto: Penguin, 1994.

Davidson, Alistair. *Antonio Gramsci: Towards an Intellectual Biography*. London, UK: Merlin, 1977.

De Maillard, Jean. *Le marché fait sa loi.* France: Mille et une nuits, Dpartement de a Librairie Artheme Fayard, 2001.

De Montaigne, Michel. *Complete works: essays, travel journal, letters*. Stanford, Ca: Stanford University Press, 1957.

Francis, Diane. "Immigration sponsorship policy a disaster – $1 billion annual tax bill for taxpayers as relatives opt out." *Edmonton Journal*, March 14, 1999.

Fukuyama, Francis. *The End of History and the Last Man*. New York: Free Press, 1992.

George, Susan. "Winning the War of Ideas." *Dissent*. Summer, 1997.

Jarmusch, Jim. *Dead Man*. Alliance/Miramax, 1996.

Loriggio, Francesco. *L'Altra Storia: antologia della letteratura italo-canadese*. Monteleone, Italy: Vibo Valentia, 1998.

Mack, Maynard et al. (eds.) *Norton Anthology of World Masterpieces, Volume 1, fifth edition*. New York: Norton, 1985.

Metaxas, Yiannis. *Abuse of Forms*. Athens, Greece: Kastaniotis, 2003.

Orwell, George. *1984*. New York, NY: Harcourt Brace Jovanovich. [1949], 1983.

Ralston Saul, John. *Voltaire's Bastards: The Dictatorship of Reason in the West*. New York, NY: Free Press, 1992.

Reid, Scott. "Survival According to Atwood." *National Post*, Saturday, April 10, 1999.

Ricci, Nino. *Lives of the Saints*. Dunvegan, On: Cormorant, 1990.

Saul, John Ralston. *Voltaire's Bastards: The Dictatorship of Reason in the West*. New York, NY: Free Press, 1992.

Thurow, Lester. "Only big investors thrive." *International Herald Tribune,* July 24, 2002, p. 6.

Printed in October 2005
at Gauvin Press Ltd., Gatineau, Québec